MW01124888

The

# Gift

in

# Every
# Day

*Little Lessons on*
*Living a Big Life*

DAVID AVRIN

SOURCEBOOKS, INC.
NAPERVILLE, ILLINOIS

Published by Sourcebooks, Inc.
P.O. Box 4410, Naperville, Illinois 60567-4410
(630) 961-3900
Fax: (630) 961-2168
www.sourcebooks.com

Library of Congress Cataloging-in-Publication Data
Avrin, David.
 The gift in every day / David Avrin.
   p. cm.
 ISBN-13: 978-1-4022-0741-9
 ISBN-10: 1-4022-0741-7
 1. Conduct of life. I. Title.

BJ1581.2.A78 2006
170'.44--dc22

                                      2006014428

          Printed and bound in the United States of America
             LB   10 9 8 7 6 5 4 3 2 1

For Sierra, Sydney, and Spencer—who I'm doing it all for.
And for my amazing wife Debbie—who I'm doing it all with.

# Acknowledgments

The people who have impacted my life and, in turn, contributed to this book are too numerous to mention. For those directly involved, I give thanks to my editor at Sourcebooks, Deb Werksman, for believing in this book. To my astoundingly straightforward and knowledgeable literary agent Jody Rein. To Jennie Shortridge for your invaluable help with the proposal. To my brother Eddie Pells, the two-time Associated Press sportswriter of the year, for helping me to weed out the "crap." To my sister Nicole for your creative suggestions. To Eric Chester for your contributions to this book and for your unending support and friendship. To my mom, Barbara Avrin-Gedye, for your "no-vanilla" approach to life that lives on in me. To my stepmom Maggie for telling me as a child that I was your "favorite." And to my father Philip Avrin for showing me, by your example, what it is to truly be the "Daddy." You're my hero.

And to our children: Sierra, Sydney, and Spencer. You are all beautiful, smart, talented, and so very loved. Now go do your homework. And to my amazing, stunning, and very cool wife Debbie. Thank you for our babies, our friendship, and for always rocking my world.

# Contents

"The purpose of life is to be useful, to be responsible, to be compassionate. It is, above all, to matter, to count, to stand for something, to have made some difference that you lived at all."

—*Leo Rosten*

# Introduction:
# A Quest for Impact

When I look at life, I have to see more than simply the biological distinction between those who are and those that were. I see actions and deeds and their residual effect—their impact on others and the world around them. I see their legacy. I see my legacy.

When a celebrity dies, the evening news creates a brief retrospective of their life—a time capsule, if you will, highlighting their well-documented achievements or public foibles. They often show video clips of their famous movie roles or footage of their political, musical, or athletic life in the spotlight.

But for most of us, there is no running video chronicle of our life, no published reviews or tabloids telling us whether we are currently in or out of favor with the public at large. Our "scorecard" is far less tangible.

I have to admit that I've never really struggled to find meaning in my life. What is truly important in this world seems to me far too evident to overlook or ignore. This book is not intended as a search for meaning, but rather a quest for impact: to be remembered—not for merely having been, but for having been someone to someone else.

While my mortality isn't anywhere near imminent (to the best of my knowledge) and I'm not experiencing a midlife crisis, I do find myself at a crossroads of sorts. I'm not so old as to think that time has run out on my dreams, but not so young as to think that I have my whole life ahead of me.

At forty-two, I'm basically at the halfway point—the time when many of us begin to reflect and review, to take stock, and to ask the big questions:

- Am I satisfied with my life?
- Am I living the life I intended to live?
- Am I truly making an impact?

With this book, I propose we instead ask these questions:

- When I look back at my life from old age, what do I want to see?
- What do I want to have accomplished, built, nurtured, earned, fostered, laughed and cried over, won, lost, and learned?
- When I envision a life worth living, and a life to be proud of, how should I live my life today so that I can look back without regrets?

The following pages are filled with moments, events, reflections, lessons, and dreams that together, I believe, create a life worth celebrating. Some have happened and are a part of who I am, while others I simply aspire to.

Upon reflection, I have come to realize that the experiences, small moments, and enduring lessons of every day are indeed a gift. Most have simply to be recognized to be appreciated.

While the memories and musings in this book are mine, I hope that in reading them you will be inspired to reflect on your own experiences and the impact you've made through your works and deeds.

I hope that they inspire you to recognize the gifts that abound in your life as well.

There's a question that I think we all ask ourselves at one time or another: "What have I done with my life to this point, and what do I want to do with the time I have left?"

I write this book not as a promise to those that I love and respect, but more as an exercise of inspection and introspection, recounting the memories that I've accumulated and have yet to create throughout the rest of my life. When I look back at my life from my later years, this is the good life that I want to have lived and hope to recall.

How am I doing? Check back with me in about forty years. I'll let you know.

—David Avrin

> "If you bungle raising your children,
> I don't think whatever else you do will
> matter very much."
>
> —*Jacqueline Kennedy Onassis*

## *I hope to be remembered for:*

- being a good role model for my kids

- being true to my wife, always

- my sense of humor

- working hard and being good at what I did for a living

- being a doting husband, father, and grandfather

- making it in the world—my own way

# Lasting Impressions

I was talking to my brother the other day about a slightly contentious family matter and one comment he made really stuck with me. He said, "Well, you know how Mom is." At that moment, I became fully aware that some day my kids will grow up and they'll talk about my wife and me just as we talk about our parents. Scary! The question is—what will they say?

I can already see it sometimes, as our daughters strategize about how to negotiate for something they want, or give each other a look that says, "Get out of Mom's way—she's pissed!"

No one knows us better than our own kids, and while they are currently legally required to be subservient to both our rational and irrational demands of them, they won't always be. They'll grow up someday and be perfectly within their rights to tune us out or simply dismiss us.

Even as our relationship with them grows and changes over the years, much of how they approach life will be influenced by how they watched us navigate our parental years.

The reality is that we get to decide, by our actions today, how our grown children will refer to us down the road and how they'll see their eventual role as parents. Will they remember us as caring, tolerant, and encouraging? Or will they remember us as impatient, perfectionist, and harried? Will we be the ones who put the word fun in dysfunctional?

I have memories of my mom getting very flustered over spills at the dinner table. My youngest sister was a bit of a klutz when she was very young and always seemed to be knocking things over, creating bad spills. Trying to diffuse the situation, the "middle child" in me would leap to my feet and announce, "Dave to the rescue!" and run to help clean up before my mom got too mad. My dad still does his impression of my sister as he waves his arms and knocks over anything in his path. Thirty years later, she is only now seeing the humor in all of this.

But today, I have a rule that says, "We don't get angry over spills." Spills happen and are seldom intentional. But the rule also says that when we spill something, we have to clean it up. I don't get angry anymore, because it isn't my problem. Eventually my kids will learn to be more careful and their motor skills will improve—just as ours did.

The truth is that significant emotional events early in their lives will stand out in their memories. It's either the very good or the very bad experiences they will recall most clearly. We can be model parents three hundred and sixty-four days a year and then if we smash just one bowl of chili into the television screen, that's all they'll remember!

The truth is we can't be perfect parents, even most of the time. But we can approach small moments with a larger vision. We can continually remind ourselves that each action can have ramifications in their memories.

When they look back, on the whole, will their glass of childhood memories be half empty or half full? "Well, you know how Dad can be." Do I?

> "Children are like wet cement. Whatever falls on them makes an impression."
>
> *—Haim Ginott*

## *As I grow older, I'm going to miss:*

- carrying my sleeping children upstairs to bed
- being able to get away with a spiky "boy-band" hairstyle
- the feeling I had when I was young that I knew everything
- the smell of my children's freshly washed hair
- my flat stomach
- believing that I had my whole life in front of me

> "My father didn't tell me how to live;
> he lived, and let me watch him do it."
>
> —*Clarence Budington Kelland*

## *When I finally go, I'd like to leave:*

- lots of pictures for and of my family
- grandchildren to carry on the family name
- a nice life insurance policy (but not too big)
- a family heirloom from my parents to my kids
- evidence of who I was, what I did, and what I stood for
- my blue lamé sport coat for a new generation of rock stars

# Because I'm the Daddy

No matter how old we get, we will always be someone's son or daughter, and if we're lucky, we also get to be someone's mommy or daddy.

I had a good friend who laughed at how her terms for her parents had evolved in her lifetime. She says her "Daddy" became "Dad" and then "Pop," followed by a brief fling with his first name. Then, when she reached her twenties, it was back to "Dad." Now she says, after thirty-five years, he's "Daddy" again.

What was interesting for me was how I went through a similar cycle with my dad as well. Now, if I call him by his first name, he just laughs at me. "Hey, Phil," I say. "Yeah, Dave," he mocks, matching my tone. And now I see it happening with my own kids. But with our oldest being just eleven years old, "No, no, no. First names don't fly in this household, young lady!" Just as names follow a familiar pattern, so do our parenting styles, as we inevitably go through much of what our parents experienced as they prepared us for the real world.

Throughout my adult life, my father has always been a good sounding board for me as I struggled with each progressive life stage. Not only has he been unendingly supportive, even as our "styles" differ significantly, but he has always helped to put things in perspective.

When I complain about having to spend six hundred dollars to replace the clutch in my car, he notes how fortunate it is that I have the money. "Imagine how terrible it would be if you needed the clutch, but didn't have the six hundred dollars," he offers. Sometimes I just want to say, "Stop being so logical. I just want to vent!"

My dad also has instilled in me an overriding protectiveness and sense of responsibility for my family. When work gets tough and I lament to my father that I'm not sure where the next client or payday will come from, I always finish by telling him not to worry. "I'll find a way to make it work," I say. "Of course you will," he responds matter-of-factly. "Because you're the Daddy. And that's what Daddies do."

He's right. I am the Daddy. I can't take a month off or fall short on the mortgage. I have a wife and three kids who depend on me. If there is a Plan B, I haven't figured it out. I think that's what fuels people's drive to buy lottery tickets. People think, *If only...*

I am not quite the pragmatist that my father is, opting instead for a much larger measure of spontaneity and entrepreneurialism. That's my nature. But when I look back, I am grateful for his example that made sure my spontaneous tendencies were tempered by a healthy dose of caution.

And some day, when my son calls to tell me about his struggles to support his family and make ends meet, I'll give him my best fatherly advice. Then I'll pause and say to him in that voice so clear in my head, "I know you'll make it work. 'Cause you're the Daddy."

"I don't deserve this award, but I have arthritis, and I don't deserve that either."

—*Jack Benny*

"A life spent making mistakes is not only more honorable but more useful than a life spent doing nothing."

—*George Bernard Shaw*

"One hundred years from now, it will not matter what my bank account was, how big my house was, or what kind of car I drove. But the world may be a little better, because I was important in the life of a child."

—*Forest Witcraft*

## *I hope I say the right thing when:*

- my daughter comes to me after getting her heart broken
- my wife asks me if her pants make her butt look big
- a police officer asks me if I know how fast I was going
- my son asks me if I ever got in trouble when I was young
- I'm offered big money to work for someone I don't respect
- I am the one at fault

# Death and Innocence

Some of the things that come out of our kids' mouths leave us dumbfounded. "Where did you hear that?" my wife will ask incredulously. "I don't know," they shrug. It's amazing what our kids will try to get away with as they mimic the "cool" new vernacular, or attempt to brush us off with some disrespectful phrase they heard on TV.

But then there are times when their innocence and naiveté is so startling and precious that you just want to hold them tight and hope they never grow up. It is these moments that form the core of my memories of my children as they grow and learn to make sense of their world. They are memories I hope I never forget.

My daughter Sydney attended afternoon preschool at the large church near our home. At four years old, she was very precocious and always inquisitive. As we approached her school one day at about noon, we noticed the parking lot was full of cars. There were long black limousines in the circle drive near the entrance and there were dozens of people in dark suits milling about outside the doors.

As I drove around looking for a place to park, Sydney leaned up from the backseat.

"Is there church today, Daddy?" my daughter asked.

"No, honey," I answered. "It looks like there's a funeral today."

"What's a funeral?" she asked innocently.

"Well," I began, struggling for the right explanation, "it's for when somebody dies. All the people who love them get together at their church and then they take turns going up on stage and saying really nice things about them like how much they love them and how they're going to miss them."

My daughter paused, looked up at me quizzically, and said, "And then they kill them?"

I blurted out an involuntary laugh and said, "No, no, sweetheart. This is for people who have already died."

"Oh," she said matter-of-factly, all of it suddenly making more sense. She then leaned over, gave me a kiss, and bounded out of the car. She looked both ways and was off to her class—skipping all the way.

I sat there in my car laughing with tears running down my cheeks for almost ten minutes.

I recounted that story for my family later and we all laughed together. "Hey, what time is the human sacrifice?" my brother asked, looking at his watch.

Despite what any of my kids go on to accomplish in their lives, when I look back, it'll be hard not to see them as they were. Sydney is something special. And while I will always love her spirit, like all my kids, I'm going to miss her innocence.

## Someday I hope I get the chance to:

- sing on stage with my kids

- mend all my fences

- properly thank my parents for all they've done for me

- renew my wedding vows

- watch all the classic old movies I've never seen

- record my parents telling me about their lives when they were young

## I want to show my kids:

- that work is called work for a reason

- lots of love and attention

- what poverty really looks like

- that you can't sit and wait for opportunity to knock

- how to lose with grace and dignity

- lots of affection for their mother

> "No legacy is so rich as honesty."
> —*William Shakespeare*

## *Good memories I have yet to experience:*

- My twentieth wedding anniversary. And my fiftieth...

- Eventually building a tree house in the two-inch-thick ash tree I just planted

- Emptying the nest and being alone with my wife— all over the world

- Retiring and sleeping in—on Monday!

- Taking my son to his first ball game (my girls already go)

- My stepdaughter growing up and thanking me for always loving her as my own

# Making Amends

The process of becoming a man can be fairly tumultuous for teenage boys. It certainly was for me. Not only did I arrogantly know everything there was to know, but I also wanted the freedom of coming and going as I pleased, while still expecting my father to pay my way. "This is not a hotel," my father would say. "You still have responsibilities as a part of this family. If you're going to live under my roof..." Well, you know the rest.

One day, shortly after my high school graduation and after a particularly vocal run-in with my dad, I made two very big errors in judgment. First, I told him to kiss my ass. Then I made the even bigger mistake of showing it to him. When I returned home later that evening to find my belongings on the front lawn, it became clear that I had crossed the line.

I bounced from friend's house to friend's house that

summer as I prepared to leave for college. Money was tight, and since I was persona non grata at my house, as my father and I were not on speaking terms, I was strapped for cash. I had a job mowing lawns for the local school district, but barely made enough to pay for the food I ate. While I had a earned a scholarship for college, I had no money for the extras—like food or clothing. As the fall of my freshman year approached, I realized that I had virtually no warm clothes that fit my still-growing body. Worse yet, I didn't even own a pair of socks.

Now you have to remember that this was the summer of 1982. One of the biggest shows on TV was *Miami Vice*, and Don Johnson was beyond cool. Don Johnson did not wear socks. Ergo, David Avrin did not wear socks. But autumn was approaching, and winters in Northern Colorado bear very little resemblance to summers in Miami. I clearly needed socks.

A good friend of mine had a sister who worked at a well-known department store and had let me in on their "little scheme." For some time they had played out this scenario wherein he would take clothes up to the register where she worked and she would pretend to ring the items up, but then would cancel the sale. She would pack the clothes in the proper bags, hand them to her brother, and say, "Have a nice day."

I had declined to participate in the scheme, but not out of any major sense of moral outrage. I was a teenager and game for almost anything, but stealing was a pretty scary proposition. Oh, I had swiped real-estate signs and salt and pepper shakers, mostly as a prank, but shoplifting was on a whole different level. I was eighteen and scared to death by the prospect of jail.

But desperate times called for desperate measures. I was two weeks from my first day of college, and I needed socks. My friend and I entered the store with two entirely different dispositions; he was confidently making his way from rack to rack, while I walked tentatively down the aisle, my heart pounding. I gathered up several packs of underwear and socks, and made my way toward his smiling sister. Just before I made it to the register, my friend stuffed two sweaters and a pair of jeans under my arm. "Are you crazy?" I said as quietly as I could. "You need 'em," he said, urging me on.

I approached the register and watched the scenario unfold, just as it had been described so many times before. I took the bag as it was handed to me and made my way to the mall exit. It was as if each step I took, the door got further away. My heart was racing as I was sure that she had inadvertently left a sensor tag on one of the pieces of merchandise. I made it to the doors and walked right through. I felt like I wanted to throw up. I was so scared that I insisted that we just get out of there and get home as soon as possible. Even as we drove to my friend's house, I was sure that store security was driving among the cars behind us and was taking down our license plate number.

Well, as you may expect, I was never caught. And while I was certainly relieved, I was never proud. To be honest with you, I don't relish the thought of my kids reading this story, but there is a larger lesson. There is a great saying: "The measure of a man's character is what he would do if he were never found out." No one at the department store knew what I did that day, but I never forgot.

And while it didn't make a significant difference to their profits, or likely affect anyone's job, I am not who I was and felt the need to make it right. There was something unresolved in my life that I had the ability to make right. So a few years ago I sat down and wrote a letter.

*Dear Mr. Chairman,*

*In 1982, when I was eighteen years old, I stole merchandise from your store. I make no excuses for my actions. Despite my needs at the time, I was old enough to know better and I knew it was wrong. And while it may have been dismissed by your company as a foreseeable loss, or chalked up to the "cost of doing business," it is not something that I can, in good conscience, dismiss myself.*

*I am now a grown man, a successful professional with three kids of my own, and am working hard to set a good example. While we all have regrets in terms of our behavior early in life, the real measure of lessons learned is what we do to make things right.*

*In that vein, please accept the enclosed check as payment for the items stolen and the cost of reconciliation. If there is no line item to apply it to, please feel free to donate it to a charity in*

*your name. I am truly sorry for what I did, and appreciate the*
*opportunity to make amends.*

*Sincerely,*
*David L. Avrin*

As in the television show *My Name Is Earl*, wouldn't it be gratifying to have an actual written list of past offenses that could be systematically checked off as we made amends, buried the hatchet, or finally did the right thing? Whether or not we've taken the time to write down our lists, we all have one. What a great feeling it would be every time I pulled out my pencil and crossed off an infraction.

There goes one right now.

## "Life is a gift. Prayer is a thank-you note."

*—Noah benShea*

### *I hope I never stop:*

- courting my wife

- believing in myself

- looking for the lesson in the loss

- being ambitious

- having faith

- rooting for the underdog

# Presence over Presents

When I was twelve years old, I remember running downstairs in my pajamas with my brothers and sisters, eager to open our holiday presents. I don't remember much about that particular year except that money was tight, as my parents were going through a bitter divorce.

I remember the look of shame on my dad's face as we tore away the wrapping paper to find used toys and games that he got from neighborhood garage sales. We kids didn't care much, but my dad was proud and unaccustomed to the recent hardships. We shooed away his apologies and dove into the gifts, but I could see the embarrassment on his face.

That holiday was a memorable one for me for another reason. That morning I received something that I had coveted for so long. My favorite gift that day, and in the years since, was my dad's old baseball glove.

It was his glove from high school and I used to borrow it all the time. It made me feel grown-up. It was soft and broken in and had some character to it. While I had my own baseball glove, nothing felt as good, or caught as well, as my dad's glove. And now it was mine.

While I know that, for my father, it was just something else he could throw into the mix, lacking the resources for more extravagant gifts for his large brood, I also know that it was a passing of the torch. I imagine it's the same feeling that women get when they're given their mother's or grandmother's wedding ring. I know what most of the women are thinking right now, but don't underestimate the value of a father's baseball glove to a young boy. I don't think I took it off for a week.

So here's the question: how many presents can you remember receiving as a child? Between birthdays and the December holidays, most of us receive many dozens—if not hundreds—of presents by the time we reach our late teenage years. Yet most of us can recall only a handful—maybe a first bicycle or a train set.

How much do we all obsess over the presents we give to our kids today? It's the latest "this" or the most popular "that." My kids open presents like they are unpacking moving boxes, barely pausing to really consider and appreciate each one. "Gotta get to the next one." It's a little sad to watch, but entirely our fault. We have decent resources and yet spoil our kids trying to keep up with the Joneses. Sometimes I think we are the Joneses.

While I certainly received many, many presents

throughout my childhood, my greatest memories were when I got to go to a movie or out to dinner alone with my dad. We did a lot of things together as a family with my many brothers and sisters, but my best memories were of "special time" with just me and my dad.

I'm not suggesting that it has to be one or the other. But I defy anyone to think of more than five presents they received while growing up. The toys were just not important enough to remember. The greatest gifts are the special times spent with the special people in our lives. And when my kids look back, I hope that they feel that presents never took the place of our presence in their lives.

## I hope I never miss:

- a performance by my kids
- the Publishers Clearing House guys at my door
- a homemade meal
- a class reunion
- the chance to refer business to a friend
- a subtle cry for help from my kids

## When I look back, I'm going to miss...

- my children believing in Santa Claus
- my thick, dark hair
- my children when they leave home
- my parents when they pass
- being cool (I already miss it)
- a noisy house

"Men show their character in nothing more clearly than by what they find laughable."

—*Anonymous*

## *I hope I never take for granted:*

- that my kids need my unconditional love and support

- that my wife needs my unconditional love and support

- the freedoms we enjoy and my responsibility to vote

- the extra time my kids' teachers put in every day, every week, every month....

- that I have food on my table, clothes on my back, and a roof over my head

- that every day is indeed a gift

# Life Happens

When I was in college, I wanted a lot out of life. I wanted to be rich and famous, with a beautiful wife and a really cool motorcycle. But surprisingly enough, even at that early age, what I wanted most was to be a father. At that time I had recently reconciled with my own father and I began to think about the kind of father I would be.

I realize now that it was all part of building "the list." At some point, most of us begin to compile a mental list of those things we want to do, acquire, or be in our lives. Making the list is one thing, but it is quite another to find yourself, years later, checking things off, eliminating items, adding new ones, and ultimately, facing your own mortality.

At this point in my life, my list is much shorter, but filled with more deal-breakers. It's fascinating how reality sneaks into your life. And it's not that you no longer have ambitions—it's just that the wants become more realistic and the needs become unequivocal.

I've been in relationships where, in the end, I felt as if I was being tolerated as opposed to being truly appreciated. I couldn't see myself being relegated to that level of companionship for the rest of my life, so I left. "Being appreciated" made its way onto the list. I would never have thought to aspire to that until it was conspicuously absent from my life.

For me, kids were also a deal-breaker. I was once in a relationship with a wonderful woman who didn't see herself having children. I told her that while I truly loved her and wanted to spend my life with her, I needed to be a father. In the end I had to choose, and today I am grateful to be a father.

Beyond the list, how many of our lives are following the script we wrote for ourselves when we were eighteen years old? Not many, I would guess. Just as Father Knows Best was more the ideal than the reality, most of our lives don't play out like a traditional Hollywood love story.

This is not to say that things don't work out in wonderful ways; it is more that there are many paths to love and life, and few follow their early script. Mine is such a story.

I dated quite a bit in my twenties and spent time with some great women. And while some relationships lasted longer than others, it was all part of the grand audition. My brother Doug called it "trying on hats." While some wondered why I wasn't settling down, Doug knew that I was looking for my future wife and the mother of my children, and that I wasn't going to settle for one that didn't fit.

We all have our mental list of desired qualities that we are seeking in a lifelong mate. While my list included many of the typical things a healthy young man is looking for in regards to attractiveness, etc., my list also included some deal-breakers. Characteristics of the "Do Not Date" list included chain smokers, "psycho chicks," druggies, the hygienically challenged, and kids. More specifically, her kids with some other guy.

Now understand, all my life I've loved kids. I was enthralled with the thought of having some. I just wanted kids of my own, and didn't want the baggage that came from her previous relationship and a lifelong connection to the "ex." I could just imagine the future teenager yelling, "You're not my dad! You can't tell me what to do!"

So I thought I had it all mapped out, but what I didn't anticipate was falling in love with a certain young lady. She was smart, funny, and affectionate. We spent hours together reading, taking walks, and watching TV. She was everything I'd always wanted and I couldn't imagine not having her in my life.

Despite my early reservations, we started spending more and more time together, and she often fell asleep in my arms. Then something wonderful and unexpected happened. I fell in love with her mother.

Sierra was eight months old when I first met her and she was four when her mother Debbie and I got married. She is my first, our oldest, and knows the special place she holds in my heart. Debbie and I have added two more since. So much for the script.

When I look back, I realize that most of us aren't living the script we imagined when we were younger. But that boring old script in my memory doesn't hold a candle to the amazing screenplay that has played out in my life.

"Everyone always says that we need more hours in the day. I think we need more hours in the night!"

—*Sierra Middlebrooks*
*(a very sleepy eleven-year-old on her way to school)*

"The words that a father speaks to his children in the privacy of home are not heard by the world, but, as in whispering galleries, they are clearly heard at the end, and by posterity."

—*Jean Paul Richter*

# Holding On

My son Spencer, the youngest of our three children, is two and a half years old, and I can't keep my hands off him. He's like a drug. He is the cutest, warmest, sweetest, softest, squishiest little boy on the planet and I can't walk by him without grabbing him and kissing him. He is my angel boy.

Coming from a very affectionate family, I've always been pretty touchy in general, but this time is different. This is my last time. After two wonderful daughters, my wife and I were blessed with a son and now we're done—surgically!

I read a quote from a woman who said that there are times when you would give everything you own just to have your grown children little again, for just a day. I understand the sentiment.

I am very affectionate with my daughters as well, but now they're getting a little too cool to play Kissy

Monster with Dad. Spencer is my last chance, and he's getting it with both barrels. And while he certainly adores his mother, he's kind of a Daddy's boy. We love to laugh and roughhouse together, and when my wife and I pull him into bed with us in the middle of night, he always slides over to snuggle with Dad. It's heaven.

Unfortunately, he's at the height now that his feet are right in line with my nether regions. I am often awakened in the middle of the night in excruciating pain. My brother Dan says that it's just my son displaying his genetic predisposition to ensure that there are no future heirs.

But unlike the affection I show for my daughters, I am taking special care to relish and remember each moment with my small boy. My wife and I catch each other getting misty when Spencer gives me a big hug and walks over to do the same for her. We just hold him tight, close our eyes, and drink him in.

The other day, I sang him a song and rocked him to sleep in his room. After laying him gently into his crib, I left his room only to find my wife, Debbie, standing in the doorway with tears in her eyes. "Just to see my two men snuggling together is so sweet," she says, choking back tears. Okay, so we're really sappy parents.

It has gone so fast with our girls and now, with our last little one, I am going to remember every snuggle, every pudgy-armed hug, and every funny word that comes out of his mouth. I am going to kiss his cheeks until a team of Clydesdales pulls me off him. It's going to be a long time before we're grandparents and I am not going to miss a minute of this wonderful time.

It makes me think of how we were once that little bundle of innocence and love to our parents as well, and how they must miss those times. As they look at us now, do they still see the squishy little babies that forever changed their lives? Do they miss it? I know I already do.

Regardless of what they become or what they accomplish in their lives, they'll always be our little babies and I hope I never forget the feeling of those little arms wrapped around my neck.

"Hey, Spencer, can Daddy have a big hug?"

## *I wish I could go back and:*

- take more pictures and videos of my brothers and sisters when we were young
- meet my wife as a little girl
- read more books
- retake all the classes I slept through
- start saving earlier
- wear my retainer

## *Good memories I have yet to experience:*

- handing my crying grandchildren back to their parents
- taking my last child to college and driving straight to the motorcycle dealership
- buying a mountain cabin with my brothers
- giving my daughters away at their weddings
- making my final mortgage payment
- getting too old to care how skinny my legs are

"Try to live your life so that you wouldn't be afraid to sell the family parrot to the town gossip."

—*Will Rogers*

## *I hope to be remembered for being:*

- one of the good guys
- someone that a friend could always count on
- a little bit larger than life
- irreverent
- optimistic
- the guy who thrilled audiences with his raucous, gyrating rendition of "Sixty-Minute Man"

# Forever and Always

I was listening to a radio talk show while driving one night and a woman called in and began telling the on-air psychologist about her dilemma. She was married with three kids and began taking a night class. "Well, there is this guy in the class," she began.

The psychologist immediately interrupted her. "Drop the class." "Excuse me?" the woman asked. "Drop the class immediately," the psychologist repeated. Before the woman could continue, the host went on to explain that she "knows where this is going" and even entertaining the thought, or the fantasy, is a slippery slope that will lead to pain for a whole lot of people.

This scenario speaks to what I like to call "the line." I've had guy friends who speak arrogantly about the line. "You can get right up to the line," they say, "as long as you don't cross it." Most of these guys are now divorced because they saw approaching the line as acceptable. They gave in to temptation. They got too close to the edge and fell. They believed the grass was greener, even if only for a night, and it destroyed their marriage.

Now mind you, I'm no Puritan. I love women. I love how they look and how they feel and smell. I'm also darn lucky that my stunning wife excels in all of these categories. But the point is that despite being a healthy, red-blooded male, I made a commitment and there is no moment of pleasure, no fantasy of perfect companionship that is worth my marriage. There is no woman alluring enough for me to risk losing my wife and being relegated to seeing my kids on weekends and every other Wednesday.

At the halfway point in my life, I've watched too many people's lives ruined by believing it was just an "innocent drink together" or "harmless flirting." The reality is that nobody's spouse can ever compete with a fantasy. That fantasy partner never had to clean up dog crap from your carpet, negotiate family bills when money was tight, or carry extra weight after delivering your child. The fantasy partner never had to put up with your annoying habits day after day and love you anyway. If the fantasy were truly better, you'd end up trading in for a new model every three years or so when the luster wore off. Yet still people stray.

When was the last time someone said, "That affair was the best thing I've ever done"? It's like drugs. You never hear, "If I had only started doing crack a few years ago, my life would be so much better."

My philosophy is that you don't approach the line. You don't even look at the line.

Lusting after movie stars or supermodels is only human, but I've learned in my life that there is no such thing as a perfect mate, just one that suits you well. It's probably a good thing that I waited until my mid-thirties to get married. All the lessons I learned with everyone I ever dated culminated in the wonderful woman I ultimately married. Every romantic relationship you're ever involved in ends, until your last one. This is my last one. My wife and kids are what I had dreamt about my entire life and now the gifts are spread out before me.

When I look to my later years, I fully intend to ensure that my first wife, my only wife, is still my wife.

"If you lived to be a hundred, I want to live to be a hundred minus one day, so I never have to live without you."

—*Winnie the Pooh*

## *When I look back, I'll thank God that:*

- my children were born healthy
- I have a strong, fun, loving, opinionated, faithful, gorgeous, creative, and imperfect wife
- my kids can spell better than I can
- I can look out my back window and see the Rocky Mountains
- I live in this time, at this place, with these people
- my brothers are my friends and my friends are my brothers

> "Success is never owned, it is rented — and the rent is due every day."
>
> —*Southwestern Company*

## *I hope I never pass up the opportunity to:*

- hold a sleeping baby
- dance with my wife (or my daughters)
- share a cup of coffee with a respected elder in my field
- go sledding
- accept a professional challenge that takes me out of my comfort zone
- catch the ice cream truck driving down the street

# Making Your Own Music

As much as we all want to believe that we make our own way in the world, we can never really escape where we came from—and I'm not referring to geographic origins. Genetically, of course, we are all equal parts Mom and Dad. But you have merely to look at the vast differences in siblings to realize that we come into this world with our own unique recipe.

While I inherited a healthy measure of pragmatism (and a furry body) from my father, my spirit came from my mom, Barbara Avrin.

My mother, with her colorful tops and bright red lipstick, is big, bawdy, and loud. "If you can't hide it, decorate it!" she says. And anyone who doesn't like it can "kiss off!" she'll say with a laugh. But the truth is, they do like it. She is the Molly Brown for the new millennium. Throughout my entire life people have always said to me, "I just love your mom. She's outrageous."

That she is. And as we all come to realize as we get older that we are who we are, and my mom makes no apologies. She has lived her life on her own terms and plans to live out her final days the same way.

In fact, she informed me the other day that she wants to die on a cruise ship. Let me rephrase that. My mom wants to live on a cruise ship, until she dies. She's got it all figured out.

She says that for the same price of a nursing-care facility, she could live on a cruise ship and see the world. "Think about it," she says. "I'd never have to cook a meal; they clean your room and make your bed for you every day. If you need something in your room, they bring it to you, and there's dancing every night!"

"What will you do with all your stuff?" I ask.

"What do I need stuff for?" she fires back. "They've got the fine china, the furniture, the linens, and any book you could ever want—what else do I need?"

She's serious. And if there's anyone that could do it, it's my mom. Barbara Avrin can take over and light up a room faster than a SWAT team. (Think Liza Minnelli, but less shy.) An introvert she is not. She'll sit down at dinner on the first night of the voyage and stand up an hour later with new best friends. And the next week, she'll do it all over again.

Is her over-the-top approach to life distasteful to some? Sure it is. But even the quiet people are undesirable to somebody. The point is that I recognize that the greatest gift I received from my mother is the permission to be who I am. And while the "gifts" I've received from my parents don't define me, just like the physical traits I've inherited, their spirit remains an integral part of what makes me, *me*.

"Success is getting what you want.
Happiness is wanting what you get."

—*H. Jackson Brown Jr.*

We build on foundations we did not lay.
We warm ourselves at fires we did not light.
We sit in the shade of trees we did not plant.
We drink from wells we did not dig.
We profit from persons we did not know.
We are forever bound in community.

—*Adapted from Deuteronomy 6, Hebrew scriptures*

# Love Comes Back

**P**art of my business allows me the privilege to speak to large audiences across the country and around the world. Throughout the year, I also attend and sometimes present at conventions for the National Speakers Association (NSA). These large and exciting events bring together some of the most renowned positive thinkers, trainers, experts, and motivators in the world. Along with all the aspiring speakers and veteran presenters, there are always a good number of old timers in attendance as well. It's good to get to know some of the trailblazers whose early work helped to define the industry.

In July of 2004, I attended a large NSA convention in Scottsdale, Arizona. On the final day of the convention was the annual awards banquet honoring the best of the best. This is where five speakers, out of the thousands nationwide, are selected for induction into the speakers' Hall of Fame. That night, my good friend Eric Chester was announced from the platform and inducted to the surprise and delight of all that know him.

At the end of the evening, as people were saying their final goodbyes, a tall, older gentleman in a white tuxedo slowly walked toward me. As I realized that he was indeed approaching me, I held out my hand to meet him. Surprisingly, he bypassed my outstretched hand and unexpectedly embraced me with a full-on, lingering bear hug.

As he released me, he turned slowly to Eric and his wife, Lori, who were standing next to me, gently grabbed her by both shoulders and held her at arms length. With uncanny warmth, he asked her if she and Eric were married. She said that they were. He then looked her deep in her eyes and said warmly but emphatically, "Do not ever leave him." As she looked at him, somewhat puzzled by his comments, he continued, "Love will come and love may go, my dear, but stay. Always stay. Because love," he said, "love will always come back."

She smiled and said, "Thank you, sir." As he slowly walked away, the gentle smile never leaving his face, Eric turned to me and asked if I knew who that was. I admitted that I did not. He said, "My friend, you've just been touched by the legendary Charles 'Tremendous' Jones."

Mr. Jones, I was touched indeed.

"You cannot do a kindness too soon, for you
never know how soon it will be too late."

—*Ralph Waldo Emerson*

"There are always flowers for those who want
to see them."

—*Henri Matisse*

# Paying It Forward

It was Homecoming in 1982. I had graduated high school the past spring and was in my freshman year of college. My girlfriend, Meredith, was still back in high school and I drove the sixty miles, like I did every weekend, this time to take her to the Homecoming dance. Yeah, like I was going to let anyone else take her!

We arrived at this very fancy French restaurant that my stepmom had suggested, and we were greeted by the maitre d' and escorted to our table. I was on a tight college budget, but knew that occasions such as this were not time to skimp. I made sure I had plenty of cash on hand to see to it that my girlfriend would be proud of her college boyfriend. Embarrassed to ask, we finally decided to order only the items that we could fully understand and had a terrific meal, including several courses.

The dance itself was several miles away and it was getting late, so I asked the waiter for the check. He stated that I was not to worry, that it had been taken care of. "Excuse me?" I inquired, not quite sure what that meant. He said that someone had thought we were a lovely young couple and had picked up the check, but wanted to remain anonymous.

We were stunned. We left a good tip and made our way to my car, not completely comprehending what had just happened. As we drove to the dance, I started getting this euphoric feeling. As she and I talked, I realized that someone must have had great memories of their high school dances and wanted to do a nice gesture for another young couple that was going through that same time. Wow! What a great thing to do. It made that evening so very memorable for both of us.

That next day I made a mental note for myself that I would do the same for someone someday. Well, needless to say, time marched on and I forgot about that night and the wonderful and generous gesture made toward an awkward teenage boy and his lovely young dinner date.

Flash forward. It's 2003 and my wife Debbie and I are eating at a pretty nice place for dinner. We were celebrating a big client contract and I was in a great mood. During dinner, Debbie points out an older gentleman dining alone across the restaurant. We speculated as to what his story might be. We surmised that he was likely a widower and was finishing his days out alone. Not knowing or caring whether our speculation was correct, I decided then and there that I was going to share my good fortune.

I motioned for our waitress to come over and asked if the old man was waiting for someone. She said that he was not and that he frequented the restaurant, always alone. I asked if she would be so kind as to bring me his check when he was through, that I was going to pay his tab this evening. She looked confused, but agreed. I also asked her to please be sure not to reveal who it was from and, if asked, just to say that someone wanted to do something nice.

As he prepared to leave, we saw him in deep discussion with his waitress across the room. He looked very confused and almost concerned at first as the waitress shrugged her shoulders and smiled. He sat motionless for a minute and then looked around the restaurant, trying to determine if a friend or someone he knew was nearby, but found none. My wife and I just stared at each other, feigning conversation.

Then something extraordinary happened. The old man's face erupted in a huge smile as he sat there in the booth just thinking to himself. Then he gathered up his coat and hat and stood to leave. With one last glance around the room, he made his way to the door—the smile never leaving his face.

When I look back, I realize that you don't have to change someone's life to make someone's day. Did you have a good day today? Then go make someone else's, too.

## *I hope I never forget:*

- that my children are always watching

- my anniversary

- that my kids need special time—with just me

- that people gave their lives so that I can live in a free country

- to call my mom on Mother's Day

- that my wife and I are not raising children, we're raising adults

## *I hope to be remembered for:*

- being very, very charming
- cooking "Daddy's Famous" something
- my happy, successful children
- being an active participant in all that I did
- finding humor in almost any situation
- never being afraid to take a chance

"A champion needs a motivation above and beyond winning."

—*Pat Riley, legendary basketball coach*

## *I'll have failed as a husband if:*

- my wife doesn't consider herself lucky to have found and kept me

- I don't write a love poem for her at least once a year

- I can't make her smile and roll her eyes at my jokes

- she is ever truly tempted to stray

- she ever joins the chorus of the "desperate housewives" that sit around complaining about their husbands

- my wife ever questions my love and devotion to our children

# Quality Time

"**D**ave," my wife calls to me across the room, cupping the mouthpiece of the phone. "It's the YMCA. They want to know if you want to coach Sydney's basketball team."

"Me?" I ask incredulously. "I've never coached before," I say quietly, but emphatically.

"They're four years old!" she retorts. "What do they know? I think you should do it." I shrug my shoulders and agree.

For some perspective, I'm 6'4" and everyone always assumes that I must have played basketball. There is a danger, of course, in confusing height with an actual ability to play the game. Just as you wouldn't assume that every obese man knows how to sumo wrestle, tall people aren't born with natural basketball ability. I am one of those unfortunate souls without that talent.

In general, I've always been pretty athletic and love

sports. I was just not very strong, having graduated high school at 6'4" and 165 pounds. I was so skinny as a teenager that I was once told by a woman that I had the legs that every woman would love to have. I did not take it as a compliment. Friends have always given me a hard time about my skinny legs. At lunch, one would say, "Hey, Dave, give me your leg, I have something stuck in my teeth." Funny? No. Bitter? Why do you ask?

One night recently, my wife and I were watching one of those plastic-surgery shows on the Discovery Channel and she said matter-of-factly, "Honey, you should think about getting calf implants." I left the room.

I prepared for my first basketball practice by creating a few simple exercises for the preschoolers and designed five simple plays involving passing, misdirection, shooting, and rebounding. I showed up twenty minutes early in my brand-new Nike warm-up suit, with a ball tucked under my arm and a whistle hanging around my neck. Coach Dave was ready to teach these kids what it was to be a basketball player. Moreover, Coach Dave was going to teach them how to be a team.

I greeted all the kids and their parents and introduced my daughter Sydney, who was almost a full head taller than everyone else on the team. "Hi, I'm Coach Dave," I said with a smile, addressing my young minions. "Has anyone played basketball before?"

I was instantly bombarded by eleven extensive and detailed stories, all delivered simultaneously and enthusiastically. When order was finally restored, I realized that any more open-ended questions would not be advisable and would likely eat up the time we had left.

After sitting down on the gym floor and letting each kid introduce him or herself, I had everyone stand up with their ball and show me how they dribble. All of a sudden it was as if each child was playing their own personal game of dodgeball. Arms were flying; basketballs were careening off their shoes; children were tripping; balls were rolling in all directions; parents were chasing balls and trying to find their children. Oh, the humanity!

You've heard the analogy that situations like this one are like trying to herd cats. Except in this case, all the cats had runny noses and attention deficit disorder, with ill-fitted shorts and uncooperative sporting goods.

I took the game plan that I had prepared out of my pocket, crumpled it up, stuffed it in my gym bag, and never looked at it again.

We went on to have a wonderful season. As there were no referees, the coaches ran the floor with the kids helping them go in the right direction and offering encouragement. There were times during the season when I looked up to find that I only had two of the five kids actually on the court as one would be in the bathroom, one would be trying to climb on Mom's lap, and one would be...actually, I'm not sure where he went.

My daughter Sydney was a great shooter, and she would always do a cartwheel in the center of the court after every basket, despite my constant and emphatic reminders that there are no cartwheels in basketball.

One of my favorite players was a precious little boy named Jack Spangler. Jack had an interesting way of playing defense. Instead of holding his arms up to block shots, Jack would adopt karate poses and make loud karate sounds, daring his opponent to approach.

Sometimes Coach Dave would lift up the small kids to help them slam dunk, and sometimes Coach Dave would carry crying players to their parents' waiting arms in the bleachers. Coach Dave had the time of his life. We shared; we cheered; we wandered aimlessly at times; we had great snacks and numerous potty breaks; we high-fived. In fact, there was a lot of high-fiveing.

Now, the guy who didn't play on sports teams as a boy is coaching his fifth team, including Sierra's basketball team and Sydney's baseball and basketball teams. Amazingly, I don't lament the loss of the evenings spent at practice, because I'm with my kids, and that is always time well-spent.

It is said that "Coach" is one of the most honorable names a person can be called. You'll never know which kids were inspired by a lesson, an admonition, or a word of encouragement. I know that I have been inspired by them.

I could have thought of a dozen reasons not to volunteer my time to coach my kids' teams, but not one of those alternative uses for my time would have meant anything near what this has for my girls and me. I thank my wife for her encouragement. By the time my son gets old enough, I might actually know what I'm doing.

And you know what else? I think my calves are getting bigger!

"The quality, not the longevity, of one's life is what is important."

—*Dr. Martin Luther King Jr.*

## *I'll have failed as a person if:*

- I took more from this world than I gave
- there weren't people in this world who were thankful for my impact on their lives
- I didn't share the blessings that have been bestowed on me
- I didn't live up to my God-given potential
- I burned my bridges
- my handshake or my word wasn't as good as gold

# Touch and Go

I have been known to poke fun at pithy little sayings on embroidered pillows, printed posters designed for teenage girls' rooms, or coffee mugs. "Don't walk in front of me, for I may not follow..." or "Love is like the waves of an ocean..." Yuck. It's like greeting cards exploding all over your home.

But I do have to admit that one has stayed with me over the years. It is the one that talks of friends coming in and out of your life. To paraphrase, it says that some come and go quickly while others touch our lives and we are never the same again.

Think about the tens of thousands of people you've met in your life. How many of their names can you recall? How many do you really know? How many would you call friend, and how many do you feel truly connected to?

When I was in college, I was a resident assistant in the dorm. One of my good friends on staff was a girl named

Annette Bighley. I called her Funicello, or often just Chello. We were very different and probably would not have met or been friends had it not been for the circumstances of our employment and residence. I don't know that we ever hung out outside the confines of the dorm, but on campus we were great friends and a good support system for each other. I teased her often, as was my nature, while she shook her head and laughed at my over-the-top approach to life. Mostly we laughed and talked till the late hours.

She was majoring in sign language and had dreams of interpreting on Broadway. Our relationship was totally platonic. She was a sweetheart and very easy to be around. For that time in our lives, something just fit. She was my dear friend.

Well, as is too often the case, we went our separate ways after college, and I didn't hear from her for years. One evening she called from her home out of state, and we had a wonderful conversation about our college years and our lives since. At the end of the call, I paused, pondering the standard, "Great to hear from you, let's keep in touch," and instead decided to tell the truth.

I said, "It has been so great to hear from you, and I while I'd like to say 'Let's keep in touch,' the truth is that life is busy and we probably won't. So if I don't get the chance to talk to you again, I just wanted you to know that I think you are one of the truly wonderful people in this world and I wish you all the success and happiness you can stand!"

She said that she was touched, and I said that I meant every word. Then she was gone.

The truth is that most of us have had dozens of friends in our lives, but keep in touch with relatively few. We are all a product of everything—and everyone—we've experienced. While I have very little time now to keep up long-distance friendships, when I look back, I hope to find that I had made the effort to express my heartfelt appreciation to those who have touched my life. They are all a part of who I am today. Thanks.

"As far as we can discern, the sole purpose of human existence is to kindle a light of meaning in the darkness of mere being."

—*Carl Jung*

## *Someday I'd like to:*

- host my own talk show
- be able to make a sizable contribution to charity
- compete on *Jeopardy!*
- come across someone in a coffee shop reading this book
- not worry about money
- sleep—just sleep

"I don't know the key to success, but the key to failure is to try to please everyone."

—*Bill Cosby*

"Maybe there is no actual place called hell. Maybe hell is just having to listen to our grandparents breathe through their noses when they're eating sandwiches."

—*Jim Carrey*

# Bigger Than Life

In the phenomenal, heartwarming book *The Time Traveler's Wife*, Henry DeTamble travels back and spends a great deal of time with his younger self. He acts as a mentor over the years to his five-, eight-, and eleven-year-old self, teaching him how to navigate a challenging and often intolerant world. I can identify with Henry to a large degree because I too spend a great deal of time face-to-face with my younger self. That self is my six-year-old daughter Sydney.

It is said that love is not divisible. We love all of our children 100 percent, just differently. And it's true. But I feel a special affinity for Sydney, a special protectiveness that comes from a certain level of clairvoyance. I know the world she will encounter and the barriers placed before children like her who are bigger than life. Sydney is so much like me and she approaches her world just as I did.

Friends and family have said that Sydney is my pay-back for how challenging I was as a child. If that's true, then she is my reward as well—my reward for successfully navigating the tumultuous waters of a dichotomous world that celebrates personal achievement in adults while discouraging individuality in its children.

For Sydney, as it was with me, all the world is a stage, and we are simply her supporting cast. Ever since she was born, Sydney never simply "was." She always was something—and usually it was an extreme. Even as an infant, she was either incredibly happy or extremely angry, obsessively curious or tragically despondent. Today she is a brilliant, creative, and very silly six-year-old girl who is in permanent four-wheel-drive mode.

I was the second oldest of six kids and always fought for my moment in the spotlight. In doing so, I am told that I often found that negative attention was better than no attention at all. So it is with my little Sydney. She knows everyone's hot buttons and has no qualms about pushing them. My father tells me that he was so worried about my antics as a young boy that he thought I'd ultimately end up on every illegal drug known by age fifteen. It never happened. In my teenage years, I found a way to channel that creative energy through humor, theater, and music, and Sydney will find her way as well.

Sydney is simply a bigger-than-life kid. When she tells you one of her elaborate stories, she makes you want to reach out and grab her lips with your fingers and just kiss 'em. When she's jumping back and forth from one couch to the other holding a bowl of cereal, you just want to strangle her.

So many of her over-the-top qualities drive her mother crazy, but I see the payoff down the road. They paid off for me. "Boring kids become boring adults," I say. "We could handle a little boring around here once in a while," my wife shoots back.

I can see Sydney's future school report cards in my mind: "Very bright and creative," they will say, but add, "has to be reminded to stop talking." These are the comments in the tattered, yellowing report cards in my scrapbooks.

I know I was a challenge to my parents. When I was young, all my friends would sing "Happy Birthday" to me and when they yelled, "Make a wish!" my mother would always chime in, "Why don't you wish that I let you live until your next birthday?"

As with all our kids, the goal is to help them become who they were meant to be. There is so much temptation to push the mute button a little too often, or hold too tight onto the reins. Some kids just need a little more slack than others.

Sydney is destined for greatness. I believe that one day the world will write books about Sydney and her accomplishments. For the time being, those books tend to be how-to books on parenting, like *Personality Plus*.

When I look back, I hope to find that I set good boundaries, but didn't hold onto the reins too tightly.

Like plants, children need room to grow, and some kids need more room than others.

So, today I say this—from one second child to another: "Sydney Shaina Avrin, my daughter, my love, I am your father and I come to you from the future. As you grow, just know that it's going to be tough finding your place at times and you're going to feel frustrated and impatient, but remember this: average never built anything important. Average never discovered anything, created anything, or inspired anything. Be who you are. Be bigger than life and there's nothing you can't do. And that sound you hear? That's your dad, your biggest fan, cheering from the sidelines."

## Just once, I want to:

- fly first class

- cash a check for a million dollars

- stop worrying about my kids

- eat a bucket of deep fried food and not pay for it the next day

- help build a Habitat for Humanity house

- get the old band back together for one last show

## I hope I keep:

- old love letters to and from my wife

- all the handmade Father's Day cards from my kids

- recordings of my kids when their voices were very small and sweet

- my boyish, playful nature

- quiet when my kids need to learn something for themselves

- my sense of humor, optimism, style, and purpose

"The key to realizing a dream is to focus not on success, but significance—and then even the small steps and little victories along your path will take on greater meaning."

—*Oprah Winfrey*

## *I'll be really proud:*

- to dance with my daughters at their weddings

- when my son is able to carry on the family name

- that I recorded a CD with my "band"

- to have been someone's husband and someone's daddy

- if I am ever debt-free

- to have built a marriage that lasted the ages

# The Living Years

**W**ell-known youth speaker Ed Gerety asks his young audiences these provocative questions: "If you had one hour to live, who would you call? What would you say? And why haven't you done it?"

There is a part of me that acknowledges that time is finite, obligations are many, and that there are just some things that we'll never get around to. That same part says, "If something else took priority over a desired accomplishment, then it just wasn't that important. We all have to make choices. Just let it go."

But what are those things that are worth finishing, revisiting, addressing, and resolving? Is it finishing a college degree, ensuring that your estate is in order, or making amends in a long-running dispute? At what point do we say "Que sera, sera," and when do we acknowledge that the lost opportunity would undoubt-edly cause great regret? What are the criteria?

Clearly it is different for different people, but I think the one common characteristic of justification for resolution is one's legacy. I ask myself the question, "Would not resolving this issue or not completing this task adversely affect others' recollections about me? Despite all that I have done in this life, would loved ones be disappointed in my not having reached this goal?"

I'm not suggesting that you let the perceptions of others control how you live your life; I'm merely stating that for me, I don't want to die with regrets about unfinished business.

I pity people who died never having finished the book they wanted to write, never having reconciled with an estranged parent or child, or never having been able to restore the half-finished car sitting in the garage. What a nice legacy they would have left if they had written a book for future generations, made amends with loved ones, or handed down a classic car to grateful sons and daughters.

There have been a slew of movies in recent years featuring tearful deathbed reconciliations. Fathers and sons, mothers and daughters, all saying "I'm sorry" right before the end. It makes for good theatrical drama, but also for a pretty tragic life. On one hand there is a peace that comes with receiving closure and forgiveness, but waiting until the end of life robs everyone of years of living, loving, and being loved back.

When I was in college, a friend told me about a class she was taking called Death and Dying. One night she returned to the dorm after a particularly emotional evening class. She told me about the exercise that left her and many of her classmates shaken.

In the exercise, they were each given a small candle and a lighter and told to go find a quiet spot in the classroom to be alone. The professor then began his instructions.

"What you have in your hand is a two-minute candle," he said. "Across from you is your father. When I say 'go,' you are to light your candle. When the candle goes out, your father is dead. You have two minutes to say everything you've always wanted to say to him. Go."

By the end of the exercise, there was audible weeping throughout the room. My friend was quite upset. Even telling me of her experience, she became quite emotional.

That story stuck with me and helped me to realize that I had some changes to make in my life. I was estranged from my father at the time, following a few too many run-ins as I struggled to become my own man after high school, and we hadn't spoken much in a few years. Both of us were seemingly too proud to make the first effort, or maybe he was just waiting for me to stop being such an ass.

One evening, as his birthday approached, I sat in my dorm room and wrote him a letter. It was the hardest letter I've ever written and one that most people never write. I laid myself bare. I told him how much I loved him and how much I wanted him to be proud of me. I wrote how sorry I was for the conflicts that we had had in the past. I told him that I wanted to start over and not look back with regrets that we had waited too long to bury the hatchet.

A few days after I mailed the letter, I got a call from my dad. He said, "To be honest with you, I cried when I read it."

"Well, Dad," I said, choking back tears, "I cried when I wrote it."

That was the beginning of a great conversation and great relationship that lasts to this day.

Every day, opportunity is knocking to mend fences, heal old wounds, and rebuild bridges. When I look back, I hope I don't find that I let any of these time-sensitive opportunities pass me by. Isn't there a letter you've been meaning to write?

## I'll be perfectly happy even if I never:

- ran with the bulls in Pamplona, Spain
- skydived
- climbed anything taller than my house
- appeared on a reality-TV show
- won the lottery
- became famous

## I hope I never pass up the opportunity to:

- drop money in the Salvation Army kettle
- tell my kids how proud I am of them
- change the batteries in my smoke detectors
- buckle up my kids
- buy anything a kid is selling for a school fund-raiser
- take a stand for what I believe is right

"While we have the gift of life, it seems to me that the only tragedy is to allow part of us to die—whether it is our spirit, our creativity, or our glorious uniqueness."

—*Gilda Radner*

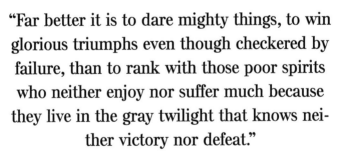

"Far better it is to dare mighty things, to win glorious triumphs even though checkered by failure, than to rank with those poor spirits who neither enjoy nor suffer much because they live in the gray twilight that knows neither victory nor defeat."

—*Theodore Roosevelt*

# Lasting Friends

I don't have many good buddies anymore. It's not that I'm not a great guy. I am. Or that guys think I'm uncool. Quite the contrary. It is merely a function of being forty-something and male. Men, as a rule, just don't have as many good friends as women. We tend to have many business acquaintances, people we work with, clients we call on, and guys in the neighborhood, but—if we're lucky—one or two good buddies.

A very insightful book from the early 1970s called *The Hazards of Being Male* referred to this condition as "the Lost Art of Buddyship." I recall that one of the chapters describes how little boys grow up hanging out with their buddies. They ride bikes together, play in the dirt together, play sports together, and get in trouble together. The primary socialization for the first fifteen or so years of their life is from other guys. So when it's time to date, boys are basically clueless about girls. We know a lot about how good girls look and how they make us feel, but very little about how to relate to them.

As we begin to date, the "great transition" begins. As we spend more time with girls, the pressure to give up our guy friends begins in earnest. We spend most of our free time with our girlfriends and are discouraged from, and even criticized for, the occasional guys' night out or the Sunday spent watching the game with our buddies.

Women will always have their girlfriends. The little-girl tea parties make way for sleepovers and ultimately the "ladies who lunch," or the moms' groups. I do recognize, of course, that many—if not most—women work both in and out of the home. But men in general work during the day and then come home in the evenings for family time. Weekends are filled with our kids' sports, household repairs, yard work, and other tasks on the "honey do" list. Little time is left for "guy time," and I miss it.

And while there are certainly major time constraints on women as well, with millions of women pulling double-duty, I'm not suggesting that the male situation is necessarily worse—just different. Some women will dismiss "guy time" simply as time to be Neanderthals—sitting around scratching and farting—but that strikes me as a bit unfair. There is just something to the male condition that only other guys can understand, a certain *esprit de corps* that comes from knowing what it is to be a guy.

Whether it's old veterans spending the afternoon telling war stories at the VFW or buddies playing on some recreational sports league together, guys thrive when feeling connected to other guys.

When I see a professional athlete getting choked up at his retirement speech, I know much of his sadness is the looming loss of camaraderie. Police officers and fire-fighters talk of putting their lives on the line for their buddies. Wounded soldiers are often eager to return to the battlefield to fight alongside their "brothers."

I occasionally come across an old buddy and it always brings back the memories of the "free and single" days. Not simply as it pertained to girls and dating, but as it relates to being free to be a guy—with other guys. But as we reminisce about the old days and catch up on our lives, there is always the unspoken understanding that we have moved on and any renewed friendship could never be as it was. There just isn't time anymore. Life is full with family and work—as it should be.

As I grow older, I hope to find that I still have a couple of good buddies from the old days. Buddies that will still give me a hard time for trying to convince the world that I am a responsible, articulate professional and father of three. They'll remind me, and anyone who'll listen, that I'm the guy who used to jump ramps on my bike, blow snot bubbles, make prank phone calls, and throw wet, sticky Milk Duds at the movie theater screen.

I miss my buddies.

> "When an old man dies,
> a library burns to the ground."
>
> —*African Proverb*

## *I realize that I'm already too old:*

- to get really big and muscular
- to learn to play the piano (well)
- to go to Cancun for spring break
- to wear cool clothes
- to play rock star anymore
- to be considered "hot" by anyone under thirty

# Voices of Experience

Following the success of *Schindler's List*, Steven Spielberg took some of the profits, created a private foundation, and set about recording the personal testimonials of as many aging Holocaust survivors as could be found before they passed away. Despite the numerous films and other notable achievements of his life, history will likely regard this body of work as Spielberg's greatest accomplishment.

But how many millions of other personal stories are lost every year as our parents or loved ones pass away? Despite the countless recording, filming, and videotaping of life's special occasions that has gone on for decades, most of the truly important events that make up our lives are never preserved, except in our memories. The lessons learned from mistakes and missteps, the humor brought about by ironic happenstance, and the hilarious questions posed by our young children learning to make their way in the world are relived only in the memories we share and the stories we tell.

Never before in history have we had such an opportunity to chronicle our experiences. Today everyone is armed with a video camera. From wild police chases to almost every birthday party on the planet, we are documenting our every move like never before.

Can you imagine if some of the most significant events in recent human history happened today? We'd have them recorded from every possible angle. Think of significant biblical events, building the Great Wall of China, early presidential debates, the sinking of the *Titanic*, or the signing of the Declaration of Independence. We wouldn't have to simply rely on the words in a history book or the lecture of a teacher—we'd watch it and see for ourselves.

We have this opportunity with our families as well. Consider all the times we get together for holidays, birthdays, weddings, and so many other occasions. I know with my large family, so often we sit around and tell stories, and laugh for hours—ribbing each other, disagreeing over how things actually occurred, and laughing all the way. Wouldn't it have been great if we had a video camera mounted in the corner of the room, capturing all the laughter for posterity?

Along with the scrapbooking, album making, picture taking, and video taping that goes on in our households every year, what if we spent some of that time recording our personal stories? Whether simply on audio tape or full-blown digital video, what if we set aside a day a few times a year to gather loved ones together and simply tell the stories of our lives and share memories of our youth?

Imagine these stories, punctuated by the laughter of family members who recount the same stories from their unique vantage point. What a treasure it would be to document those precious experiences. Think of future generations being able to share in those memories while gaining real insight into the humanity of those who came before them—not just the birthday parties and trips to the Grand Canyon. Think of loved ones who may be in their twilight years. What do you have to remember who they truly were—and not just what they've done?

My father has told me stories of his parents coming to America. My grandfather was a poor Russian tailor. His first job in America was making uniforms for the U.S. Olympic team in Los Angeles in 1932. My dad told me of his difficult relationship with his own father, how he joined the army, and of his adventures as he traveled throughout Europe.

He's told me hysterical stories of raising us six kids and the difficult times following the divorce with my mom. He tells us of the brutal custody battle, and how, in the end, he "lost" and had to take us, he says with a smile. So many stories, yet all are simply housed in his aging memory—and mine.

Wouldn't it be wonderful to hear my mom and dad tell us their stories in their own words and in their own voices, to be played long after they're gone?

I want to look back at the end of my life and know that time didn't run out. I need to record those memories of my parents for my kids, my wife, and myself. I need to record my life experiences and those of my wife for our children, grandchildren, and for whoever else may care. We all have the means to leave a true record of ourselves and our loved ones in our own words.

Charge the batteries and hit the Record button.

"I was a young person once, shortly after the polar ice caps retracted, and I distinctly recall believing that virtually all adults were clueless goobers."

—*Dave Barry*

## *Someday, I think it would be fun to:*

- live overseas for a year
- arrange all the home movies in chronological order
- spend a week traveling with each of my kids separately
- lie in bed with my wife for an entire weekend watching the movies that we missed while raising our kids
- hang out with my son just being "guys"
- share the love letters to and from my wife with my kids

"That best portion of a good man's life—his little, nameless, unremembered acts of kindness and of love."

—*William Wordsworth*

## *When I finally go, I'd like to leave:*

- good family traditions
- this world before my children (nobody should have to bury a child)
- many funny stories for family to share
- a little hint of myself in my kids
- the toilet seat up for a change
- no unfinished business

# Digging Around

I stumbled upon a television show the other day called *House Detectives*. The program features recent homeowners of older homes searching their home to find artifacts and other clues as to who used to live there.

As they examined small items discovered from storage rooms, attics, and behind secret panels, they speculated as to what kind of life the previous owners lived and what ultimately became of them and their descendants. While the host of the show and the homeowners were all very excited about discoveries, in an odd way, I found it somewhat sad. An entire life, or generations of full lives, reduced to a teacup, a letter from a friend, or an old doll found in a basement.

Who were these people? What were their victories and tragedies, their triumphs and regrets? Is there someone today who tells the stories of their lives to their descendants? Or are they merely, as the host energetically suggests, "interesting clues for curious house detectives?"

It's discomforting to think that my life someday might be reconstructed through a few select items from my home. Wouldn't it be great if we could somehow pre-select those items that survive the years? Maybe we'd choose photo albums, awards, or even some sort of video record of our lives. But just my luck, archeologists will dig through my home site and find a plunger or a wrench. "Hmm. The owner of this land must have been some sort of plumber," they'll say.

Maybe it's too much to ask that the countless people that die every year be immortalized in some detailed way. And why is it so important that they are remembered anyway? Don't we have a greater responsibility to this world than just inheriting it and building upon it? Maybe it's the fear of being forgotten that drives people to seek a more tangible personal legacy.

But the reality is that millions of people are perfectly happy living quiet, productive lives. Most hardworking people aren't destined ever to have their names on buildings or up in lights. Then there are those of us who can't help wanting to be remembered, to live on in some more significant way. I guess it is up to each of us to decide what we want our legacy to be and to live in a way that brings it to fruition.

When I look back, I sincerely hope that I make a more significant impact than merely the coffee mugs I leave behind for someone to dig up. I want to do important things in this life and raise self-confident children who grow up to make a positive impact of their own. What will I leave behind? What will be my legacy? Where did I leave that plunger?

"Before you criticize people, you should walk a mile in their shoes. That way, when you criticize them, you're a mile away, and you have their shoes!"

—*J. K. Lambert*

"If I had my life to live again, I'd make the same mistakes, only sooner."

—*Tallulah Bankhead*

"A friend is one who walks in when others walk out."

—*Walter Winchell*

## *Random things I'm thankful for:*

- buffalo wings
- the sound of my children laughing
- really smart doctors
- unsolicited hugs from my kids
- Singapore Airlines
- late-night fast-food drive-thru
- the pause button on my TiVo

# Connected for Life

I want to tell you a story about a good friend of mine. This is not a trick story where in the end you find out that the "friend" is really me. It's truly about him, his good nature, and his kind heart.

Mark was from a very small town in Oregon, and from the time he was small, he dreamed of leaving his community and making it in the big city. Most people were involved in the logging industry where he lived, but that kind of work never suited him, and he was determined not to follow the inevitable path of his fellow classmates.

My friend Mark had something that most of them didn't. He had talent. Mark had a phenomenal singing voice and he came to realize that his voice might be his ticket out. One day he auditioned for a large gospel singing group that was traveling through town. They were so impressed with his talent that they offered him a spot in the group. He had unfinished business at home, but eventually found his way to the group and with them traveled around the world singing for many years.

He met and fell in love with a wonderful girl while on tour. They eventually married and had a daughter. It was everything he had ever wished for, but dark days followed. While his daughter was his greatest source of pride, his dissolving marriage was the source of his deepest pain. He and his wife separated and both struggled with the daunting task of rebuilding their lives apart while shielding their daughter from the conflict.

Still feeling great love for each other, they maintained a strong friendship in the years that followed. She went on to remarry, which was very difficult for Mark, not simply because she now officially had moved on, but because she married a guy who had been close friends with both of them. He knew he couldn't dictate who she ultimately fell in love with, but it was hard nonetheless.

Not only had that chapter of his life formally closed, but he was now relegated to sharing his precious little girl with her mom's new husband—his old friend. A year later the new couple had a daughter of their own; Mark wondered if he would crumble under the weight of it all.

But a new dynamic had entered the equation. As close as the new husband was to Mark's daughter, Mark found himself growing very close to their young daughter as well. He knew at that point that he had a decision to make. He could carry the resentment and hurt that had plagued their relationship in the years since the separation, or move past it and embrace a new paradigm—one that included a new definition of "family."

Realizing that all of them were connected for the rest of their lives, Mark offered an olive branch and they all sat down to work through the differences and commit to build a bigger "family." Today they share their lives as they share their children. They all attend soccer games, school plays, band concerts, student-teacher conferences, and even some family vacations—together. They are all family—together.

While this story isn't about me, it is true that Mark's ex-wife and the mother of his daughter is now my wife and the mother of my kids. I have loved his daughter, Sierra, since she was eight months old, and Mark has always loved my daughter, Sydney, and now my son, Spencer, as well. He has been there for them since the day they were born and they are all connected. In fact, they love their Uncle Marky so much that they have never questioned for a moment that he is part of their family, as they are a part of his.

Last year, our oldest daughter Sierra brought home an essay she wrote for a fifth-grade writing assignment and stood in the kitchen and read it for Mark, Debbie, and me. Here's an excerpt:

> *Many people have done many kind acts for me in the past, but one really stands out. The one that stands out is that my parents love me enough to work out their differences to be out-*

*standing friends for the rest of our lives.*

*It makes it a lot easier for me, and they were willing to give a lot, just for me. If I were in front of them right now, I would thank them with all my heart. I would definitely want them to know how much it meant to me and I thank them so very much.*

*If I could, I would do everything I could for my parents. My parents have done such a kind act for me, and Mom, Dad, and Dad—I love them all so much.*

Needless to say, she got an A.

It is said that parents would step in front of a speeding car to save their children, yet so many find it hard to swallow their pride long enough to try to resolve problems with their child's other parent. We would all give our lives for our kids, so why is it so hard for many of us to do a much simpler thing and settle our differences—for the children?

When I look back at everything we've gone through, I am humbled by the courage shown by a good friend as he offered friendship and reconciliation, despite his pain. But when I look back, I also find myself looking ahead to the peaceful, nurturing years to come and envisioning the healthy kids we will be sending out into the world.

Thanks, Mark. I love you, man.

## *If I had more time, I would:*

- read more books
- complete my ever-expanding "honey do" list
- give my wife more breaks from the kids and let her have some more "me time"
- catch up on all the TV shows I've recorded
- give more undivided attention to my kids
- sleep—just sleep

"Never raise your hand to your children. It leaves your midsection unprotected."

—*Robert Orben*

*I would love to someday buy:*

- a player grand piano
- a beach house for my wife
- a really, really nice suit
- tuition at any college where my kids are accepted
- really good power tools
- beautiful (yet reasonable) weddings for my daughters

## I hope I never:

- have to wear a Speedo
- say something to my wife that I can't take back
- wear black socks with sandals
- need bladder-control diapers
- take my kids' "medicine" for them
- have to watch Barney again—ever!

# Pride and Prejudice

There are moments in all of our lives where events transpire in such a way as to make a profound impact on who we are and how we view the world. In the best of all instances, these lessons come at the hands of our parents, who ensure that what is learned is what is necessary for our growth. Mine came at the hands of my father, and the lesson has shaped me to this day.

My father grew up in East Los Angeles during the 1930s and early 1940s. It was a tough neighborhood, to be sure, but even more so for a young Jewish boy. A decided minority in his own community, he was too frequently the victim of gang violence at the hands of the local ethnic community.

If there was anyone who had the right to harbor prejudice against those who did him harm, it was my dad. But quite to the contrary, if he had any deep-seated prejudice, he never showed it. Throughout the years of my childhood, my parents made it clear to my brothers, sisters, and me that prejudice and intolerance would not be tolerated in our household— period! Despite the persistence of such views in society at large in those days, we were taught that neither the words nor the attitudes were even remotely acceptable.

Those lessons were made all the clearer on a summer evening when I was just twelve years old. I was playing football with a bunch of friends out on the large greenbelt between the rows of our townhouse complex. During a particularly heated exchange between my best friend Eric and me, I went somewhere that I knew I shouldn't. Lacking any semblance of a creative vocabulary, my twelve-year-old mind reached down to a shallow place and pulled out the "N" word.

The fact that my friend Eric was black was meaningless to me during the months of our budding friendship. I played at his house and he played at mine. We were buddies at school and we were buddies at home. Like all young boys, we wrestled and chased each other, talked about girls, and played lots of sports. Sometimes we quarreled. Today was one of those times.

The minute the word left my mouth, I knew I had crossed a big, big line, but we were both too mad to dwell on it. The game went on and eventually everyone made their way home.

I'm not quite sure how my father found out what I said. Perhaps my brother had told on me. But all I remember is the door to my bedroom flying open and my father standing in the doorway—his face was red with rage.

After some brief shouting and an ultimate admission of guilt, I found myself being dragged by the back of my neck up the sidewalk toward Eric's house about one hundred yards away, barely keeping my feet beneath me and crying the entire way. The neighborhood kids began to gather to see what the commotion was all about.

When we reached Eric's home, my father rang the doorbell and to my horror, he asked that Eric's entire family come outside and join us on the front porch. Then he made me apologize to each and every member of his family for what I said. He then walked me home and grounded me for good measure.

Beyond the obvious behavior modification created by the events of that day, a deeper change happened within me. By his actions my father said to me, in no uncertain terms, "This is what we believe. This is what we find acceptable. And this is what will not be tolerated."

When I look back at that evening, I see it as a significant moment in my growth as a human being. It was a lesson born of humiliation exacted upon a young boy, by a wise and benevolent father hell-bent on raising his kids to be people of integrity.

When I am inevitably confronted by a similar situation with one of my children, I hope that I will have the same courage and wisdom to react just as swiftly and harshly—and just as wisely. I believe that my children's very souls depend on it.

"Behind every successful man, you'll find
a woman who has nothing to wear."

—*Harold Coffin*

*Things I hope my kids will someday say about me:*

- "I can tell him anything"
- "I just want to make him proud of me"
- "If I don't know, I just call my dad"
- "He's really good to my mom"
- "He's always worried about me"
- "My dad is my hero"

"Watching your daughter being collected
by her date feels like handing over a
million-dollar Stradivarius to a gorilla."

*—Jim Bishop*

## Things that make me laugh:

- My young kids mispronouncing new words
- Almost anything inappropriate
- Deep Thoughts by Jack Handey
- Realizing that I am becoming my parents
- My brothers
- Serious moments that call for silence

# The Dating Game

Iknow the day will come, but I am dreading it nonetheless. Some day, in the not-too-distant future, a knock will come on the door, and standing there in the dim glow of the porch light will be some hormone-driven little bastard who has come to take my baby girl to God knows where, to do God knows what. Oh sure, they'll call it "just a date," but I know what it really means. Mostly it will mean that I am on my way to being replaced as the most important man in her life. Ouch.

We've got a few years to go, but the beginning of the end is just around the corner for both our daughters. My wife and I have had some serious and some not-so-serious discussions about how to handle our daughters' dating. As the second of three daughters, my wife Debbie rebelled against her overly strict father and was a bit of a wild child when it came to dating. She tells stories of sneaking out of the house, getting drunk, and being overly affectionate with boyfriends.

I am horrified. Not because I didn't do the same things—I most surely did. But I am a guy. I was the hormone-driven little bastard. As a teenager, I was the enticer, not the enticee. Looking at this scenario from the perspective of a father of two daughters is a completely different matter. A double standard? You bet your life!

But Debbie and I are in agreement about most things. We'll have to meet the boys first, of course, and they have to come to the house to pick them up in person. My horror, of course, is that some guy is going to drive up in a RV or some kind of converted campervan. Not in my lifetime, Bucko.

As he stands in the doorway, I'm going to say, "Sierra, why don't you go in the kitchen with your mother. Travis and I are going to have a little chat." She'll no doubt say, "Dad, please don't do this." "It's okay," I'll say back. "We're just going to come to a little…understanding. Isn't that right, Travis?"

Then I'll sit on the sofa and clean my gun while we talk. "You don't have a gun," my wife reminds me. "And we don't have daughters who are dating yet," I note. "A lot of things can change in the next few years."

My wife insists, with a smile, that I'm not really going to do all this. "You bet I am," I say emphatically. I tell her that it is crucial that all boys are afraid of their girlfriend's father. I say that the boy has to know that if he gets out of line, then he is going to have to answer to her dad. "I know what these boys are thinking," I insist. "Because I'm still thinking it!" My wife certainly knows that to be true.

The best story I ever heard was from a father who told of a time when his daughter started dating a new kid. The dad was a good guy, but pretty scary-looking at six foot two, two hundred and fifty pounds, with a shaved head and numerous tattoos. He said his fifteen-year-old daughter had a party at the house and invited over many friends, including her new boyfriend.

At the end of the night, the young man went to the girl's mother and politely shook her hand, saying that it was very nice to meet her. And as he turned to shake the father's hand, her dad bypassed the outstretched hand, grabbed the stunned boy's face in both of his hands, and kissed him right on the mouth. As the boy staggered back in disbelief, the dad leaned in, looked him straight in the eye, and said, "Just remember, everything that you do to my daughter, I'm going to do to you."

I'm still weighing this scenario along with several other options. It'll depend on the boy and my mood at the time.

The truth is that how our girls navigate this important time in their lives will have a significant impact on how they approach future relationships and ultimately their marriages. I know that these young suitors will find my daughters to be young women of character and integrity, with strong moral fortitude, good self-control, and clear, appropriate boundaries, just like their mother. On second thought, we'd better put bars on the windows.

We really do have extraordinarily talented, bright, and beautiful daughters, and they'll have to endure the dating years, just like we did. And when the time comes, I just hope that I will have found and demonstrated the right balance between fiercely protective father and understanding, empathetic Daddy. And if I ever do resort to buying a gun, you can bet it'll be really, really clean.

> "The difference between a mountain and a molehill is your perspective."
>
> —*Al Neuharth*

## *Things that bring tears to my eyes:*

- Writing love poems to my wife
- Pulling out a nose hair
- Packing up my kids' baby stuff for a garage sale
- Any time the young children's choir sings at church
- My kids' first day of kindergarten
- Recalling when my then four-year-old stepdaughter first asked if she could call me "Daddy"

"Experience is a hard teacher because she gives the test first, the lesson afterward."

—*Vernon Law*

*During my life, I'm glad I got to:*

- sing in a band

- marry the woman of my dreams

- be a daddy—times three

- have my moments in the spotlight

- enjoy what I did for a living

- create this written record of what I thought, felt, and believed

"Bad habits are like a comfortable bed: easy to get into, but hard to get out of."

—*Anonymous*

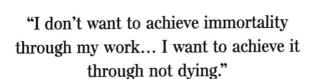

"I don't want to achieve immortality through my work... I want to achieve it through not dying."

—*Woody Allen*

> "I coulda been a contender.
> I coulda been somebody."
>
> —*Marlon Brando, On the Waterfront*

## *I'm really proud of:*

- the friendships I have with all my grown siblings

- my professional work

- my confident, creative, silly, affectionate, inquisitive children

- my optimistic, entrepreneurial spirit

- the love and friendship of my wife

- my rock-star days—long since past

# Making Your Mark

How many times have you had the chance to truly make your mark in this world? When was the last time that you were able to do something that no one else has ever done and have it documented for all eternity and for all the world to see? Well, my friends, I have had just such an opportunity, and I jumped at it.

It was the summer of 1985 and I was working at the University of Northern Colorado (UNC) in the summer housing program. After spending my first year as a resident assistant in the dorms, I decided to stay on campus for the summer and make some extra money.

During the summer months there are a couple of dorms open, serving a few students, but mostly the dorms were used for summer camps and enrichment retreats. During that summer we had sports and cheerleading camps staying on campus, and there was one group that I will never forget. That summer, UNC was host to the International Skip-Its summer camp and exhibition.

As its name would suggest, the group promoted rope-skipping as a means of exercise, but it went far beyond the simple schoolyard game. These young kids had developed some of the most intricate and athletic rope-skipping routines imaginable. They would do flips and turns and cross-overs until you were dizzy just watching them. It was truly amazing.

One day that week, the entire group headed over to the big gym on campus for the annual world-record rope-jump attempt. The leader of the group asked me to come along and help. As I arrived, the basketball court was filled with nearly 250 campers ranging in age from about six to eighteen, along with the adult staff. Also in attendance were reporters from the local paper, the *National Enquirer*, and a representative from the *Guinness Book of World Records*. Pretty heady stuff for Greeley, Colorado.

At both ends of the basketball court were A-frame ladders and a long, thick rope stretched the length of the court. The staff began lining up the kids five across, with the little kids on each end. Each row of five was subsequently added behind the next, with the tallest kids standing at half-court where the rope's arch would be the highest.

As I stood on the sideline, a staffer asked if I wanted in. I said, "Sure," and placed my tall, lanky frame squarely in the middle of the middle line right at half-court.

So there we stood, a line of "kids" running the length of a basketball court, five people across. Two of the large male camp leaders climbed the ladders at the far ends holding each end of the rope. They began to loudly count: "One, two, three!" and they whipped the rope up, around and over the group. Everyone jumped in unison. Unfortunately, the rope hit somebody's foot and collapsed to the floor. In fact, for nearly half an hour, we never managed to get past one complete turn of the rope, as at least one kid would always fail to reach sufficient height, or time the jump incorrectly.

Needing three full turns without obstruction for an officially sanctioned record, we were getting nowhere. Frustrated, the camp leaders got off the line and positioned themselves on the side with a clear view of the length of the line. Following each subsequent attempt to clear the rope, they identified and yanked the kid who inadvertently hooked the rope with their foot. While our numbers were slowly dwindling, we were still well over the number needed for an official world record rope jump.

Nearly two and half hours into the record attempt (really), our thighs were burning and the kids were exhausted. We had gotten as far as two full turns a few times and everyone was pretty ticked off at this point. Then a miracle happened: two turned into three, followed by four, five, and six. We had found our rhythm and the cheers were deafening. We all collapsed on the floor as everyone was hugging everyone. You'd think we'd just pulled a child from an underground well, or saved a beached whale and dragged it back to the sea with our bare hands. It was complete and utter pandemonium.

And in that moment, in that beautiful moment, I realized that I was part of something bigger than myself. I had been given the opportunity to make my mark in this world and I jumped. I jumped and I jumped until there was no more jumping in me! I jumped until I thought my legs would bleed and I came out a winner. I/we had done something that no one had ever done—ever! I could look back at the end of my life and know that my name would live—forever!

Of course they broke the record the next year.

"What greater thing is there for human souls than to feel that they are joined for life—to be with each other in silent unspeakable memories."

*—George Eliot*

*Before I die, I'd like to:*

- volunteer for an open-mic night at a comedy club
- host *Saturday Night Live*
- be recognized as a leader in my field
- see new treatments for many tragic diseases
- see America more respected and appreciated around the world
- write a bestseller

"If you were happy every day of your life, you wouldn't be a human being—you'd be a game-show host."

—*Gabriel Heatter*

*Words I hope are never uttered in the same sentence as my name:*

- Selfish

- Average

- Mean-spirited

- Boring

- Dishonest

- Guilty!

"Don't complain about growing old. Many, many people do not have that privilege."

—*Earl Warren, former Supreme Court Chief Justice*

## *In my final days, I'll likely think about:*

- my parents and whether they'd be proud of who I'd become
- my children, grandchildren, and my precious wife
- that incessant, annoying beeping sound from my heart monitor
- who I've loved—and lost—in my life
- who will play me in the made-for-TV movie
- my impact, my contributions, my legacy

# Before I Die

There have been so many books published in recent years listing suggested things to do before you die. These books contain some imaginative entries, including kissing under the Bridge of Sighs in Venice at sundown, dealing blackjack in Las Vegas, competing in the Iditarod dogsled race, or eating twenty Twinkies in five minutes.

While these books may make for entertaining reading, few would agree that the suggestions are a recipe for a full and rewarding life.

Tim McGraw had a terrific hit song that suggested that you should, like a terminally ill patient, "live like you were dying." But I wonder if I were made aware of my pending demise, would I have the urge to climb mountains, gorge myself on greasy foods, ride a bull, and fly to the ends of the earth? I doubt it.

I think it's analogous to a hypothetical house fire.

Most people would zero-in on family photos, scrapbooks, and home movies as items to save first. I feel the same about the value of time with my family. If I were faced with a sense of urgency regarding my time left, I would find ways to be with them.

But the reality is that I likely still have decades of time on this earth and so the question becomes more legitimate. I know what I've done so far. Now, what do I want to do with the time I have left? What do I want to accomplish before I die? Assuming my children are grown and making their own way in this world, what do I want to check off my list in the years to come?

I have to admit that most of what I still want to do are things I've always wanted to do or have done before, but have been put on hold due to family obligations. It's been a time issue and I know most can relate. I think about the days when my time was my own. I could see movies, read books, sing with my band, ride my motorcycle, lie on the couch, travel, or whatever I wanted to do—when I wasn't working, of course.

The truth is I'd like to do many of these things again. Except this time, I want to do them with my wife, Debbie. I look forward to the day when we can see every movie we want, travel to faraway places, or just lie on the couch reading a good book—together.

While I wouldn't call myself a simple person, the fact is that I don't have a long list of exotic things I want to achieve before I die. In reality, I am blessed to be doing most of what I've always wanted to do in my life and long for the opportunity and more personal time to do them more often.

When I look back, I don't think I'll regret not having run with the bulls or climbed an ice cliff, but I would regret not making time for my kids or nurturing my marriage. Some may call it simplistic, but I just see it as making a more meaningful use of the time I have left—however long that might be.

> "If you wish to be remembered, write,
> or be written about."
>
> —*Benjamin Franklin*

## *I want to show my kids:*

- how to change a tire and put oil in their car

- how to stand up for themselves

- how to find out who is really "in charge" when complaining about a product or service

- old videos of their dad as a rock star

- pictures and videos of themselves, when they were young

- how to pass up a "good deal"

## *I hope I never miss the opportunity:*

- to be on the sidelines to cheer my kids on

- to travel to somewhere I've never been

- to make out with my wife

- to chronicle, record, videotape, or take pictures

- to do something funny right at the moment my kids are drinking milk

- to reconnect with an old friend

### "There is no such thing as 'fun for the whole family.'"

—*Jerry Seinfeld*

## I would love to someday attend:

- one of my kid's medical school graduations
- the Academy Awards or the Grammys
- the Olympics
- the birth of my grandchild
- the Consumer Electronics Show in Las Vegas
- a Hollywood "afterparty"

# When It's Time

As I look ahead to what many call the Golden Years, I wonder if I'll be ready to go. It's almost a cliché at this point, but in the movies you often see elderly people on their deathbed saying things like, "I've had a good life, dear. It's my time to go." It's hard to imagine feeling that way.

In light of recent, high-profile cases, many people feel it is important to sign "do not resuscitate" orders (DNRs) where you can determine that you don't want to be hooked up to artificial life support. I'm not sure how I'll feel in forty years, or how I'd handle a debilitating illness, but for now, plug me up to everything! Hey Doc, what's that machine? Okay...uh...put it in here. I want to live!

As I wrote in the introduction, and spiritual matters notwithstanding, I'm not quite sure how people can struggle with the meaning of life. What is the meaning of anything? What's the meaning of my spatula? It just is. Is it just the vernacular, or are people really looking for the motivation to do all they need to do to feel like they are contributing or living a worthwhile life?

It's our turn to run the world. What are we going to do with it? I don't think meaning is something that is out there waiting to be discovered. We have to create it for ourselves. Impact is the end result of what we do to actively contribute. Everyone has to pull their weight. That's how we get through this whole "life" thing. And along the way, we seek out things that give us joy, making all the things we have to do seem worthwhile.

I'm not trying to be preachy, but there is so much to actively embrace. For some, it's all about work and building their business. For others, it's about adventure or advocacy work. Me? I'm just crazy about my wife and kids.

While I have great work-related ambitions, to be sure, I want to be with my family as much as possible. It goes so fast. I want to wrestle with my kids, coach their teams, and listen to their stories. I want to laugh with my wife, kiss her face, and squeeze her butt. I want to be a strong partner with her as we guide our children to becoming all they can be. I want to continue to build our relationship, beyond our roles as Mom and Dad, so that we each will have a loving companion to last us all our days.

I want to be around to see my children make their way in the world and offer support when they need it. I need to be here to see my echo in my grandchildren and know what I truly left behind. I want to be really, really old when I die. I want to stay here as long as I can to see and experience all of it.

I don't search for meaning in life. I see it in everything and I want to drink it up. We all have the opportunity to impact everything and everyone we touch. The question is, are your daily contacts meaningful ones or wasted opportunities?

Do you recognize the gifts that you are given every day, or do you too often overlook the blessings in life's little moments?

Everything matters. Everything is important. Jimmy Stewart learned that lesson in *It's a Wonderful Life*. It's not about meaning, it's about the impact we all make on the world and on each other.

Meaning is an intangible. People can always lament the lack of meaning in their life. Impact, however, is a personal responsibility. We think of the experiences we've had and will have in the time we have left, and while we can't always find the meaning, we can help determine the impact we make.

It was that quest for impact that led me to write this book, and it was through the explorations of my own experiences that I've been able to better see the impact that I've made. I guess I didn't want to wait for some horrific accident to see my life flashing before my eyes. I decided to take a look back myself and it has been an amazing journey of introspection. I've seen the good works and also where I've clearly fallen short.

When I look back on the life I've lived so far, and look ahead to the life I want to live in the time I have left, I want my legacy to be one of positive impact. I hope the people I've touched may walk a little taller and smile a little broader. I hope that, in the end, I will be remembered for leaving the campsite better than how I found it.

So here I sit with half a tank of gas still left. "Honey, kids, let's go for a drive."

"If you can give your son or daughter only one gift, let it be enthusiasm."

—*Bruce Barton*

# About the Author

David Avrin is a self-described forty-two-year-old schmaltzy husband and father of three. The second oldest of six grown "kids," David recognized early the gift of family. He is a former singer and actor, a very poor juggler, and a sports coach, business owner, and writer.

A twenty-year public relations, marketing, and branding strategist, David is a seasoned public speaker who consults with individuals and organizations about how to raise their profile in a competitive marketplace (www.visibilitycoach.com). He also records people's outgoing voice mail messages (www.recordmymessage.com).

David Avrin lives happily with his wife, two daughters, son, and dog in the Denver suburb of Castle Rock, Colorado. *The Gift in Every Day* is his first book.

## Tell Us Your Stories

If you've enjoyed this book, please take a moment and share some of your experiences as well. Go to www.thegiftineveryday.com and tell me about the lessons you've learned in your life and about your dreams for the future. You might end up in a future book.

Have comments or questions?

Write to David Avrin at: david@thegiftineveryday.com.